Park's Pantries
A Collection of Recipes to Warm Your Soul

Hinckley Park Care Home

Roswell Publishing

Text © 2023 Hinckley Park and Roswell Publishing.

The rights of Hinckley Park identified as the originator of this work has been asserted by them in accordance with the Copyright, Designs and Patents Act 1988.

All rights reserved. No part of this publication may be reproduced, stored in a retrieval system, or transmitted in any form or by any means electronic, mechanical, photocopying, recording or otherwise, without prior permission.

ISBN: 9798884865976

Cover image: Pexels @ Pixabay

For rights and other permissions, please contact Rachael at: rae@raegee.co.uk

Shelley's Sweet N' Sour Pork ... 5
Janet's Veggie Stew ... 6
Betty C's Fish Pie ... 7
David's Shepherd's Pie ... 9
John's Chicken Curry ... 13
Elaine's Cod Loins in Tomato Sauce ... 15
Mary's Steak and Ale Pie ... 16
Louise's Lasagna ... 18
Tony's Mushroom Soup ... 20
Becca's Pesto Pasta ... 23
Mel's BBQ Pork Nachos ... 24
Clive's Roast Beef with Horseradish Mash ... 26
Linda's Best Burger Ever! ... 28
Rach's Chicken and Leeks in White Wine Sauce ... 30
Kim's Roast Pork ... 33
Anne's Chicken Salad ... 35
Tree's Crispy Beef Stir Fry ... 37
Christine's Toad in the Hole ... 39
Betty T's Spanish Chicken ... 43
Brian's Roast Chicken ... 44
Asfati's Brinjal Bhaji ... 46
Betty C's Slow Cooked Liver and Onions ... 47
Asfati's Lamb Shish Kebabs ... 48
Lesley's Spaghetti Bolognaise ... 50
Barbara's Slow Cooked Rice Pudding ... 55
Betty C's Bread and Butter Pudding ... 56
Barbara's Creme Caramel ... 58
Betty C's Fruit Pie ... 59
Barbara's All Bran Loaf ... 60
Betty T's Lemon Drizzle Cake ... 63
Clive's Apple Crumble ... 64
Betty T's Victoria Sponge Cake ... 65
Richard's Rhubarb Crumble ... 67
Lesley's Eton Mess ... 68
Betty T's Gooseberry Pie ... 69

Introduction

"Cooking is like love. It should be entered into with abandon or not at all."
Harriet Van Horne

Food, for many people, is one of the highlights of the day. What more could you want than a hearty and warming meal to sit down an enjoy as the evening begins to draw in? Or a dessert that has a million memories attached to it?

Hinckley Park is a small, family friendly, care home based in the heart of the Midlands. We live in the small market town of Hinckley roughly fifteen miles south west of Leicester. While we're famous for a few things, it's the friendly locals who really make this rural town a great place to live.

Many people believe that care homes are boring and soulless places, buildings where people are left cooped up and forgotten about. We've aimed to change that and, much like the town, we're a friendly bunch who've always got a conversation at the ready and a cup of tea to hand. Food, whether we want to admit it or not, is a massive part of care home life and a good meal can make anyone happy. We're lucky to have a great kitchen team with us but we decided that we wanted to leave something for all of you. We wanted to put down our favourite foods and recipes so that when you need a pick-me-up you'll always have something to hand.

This is a wonderful little collection of cosy comfort foods, ones that we remember from our younger days or which parents and grandparents may have cooked for us. They're foods that heal broken hearts and warm cold fingers. They're foods which will always have a little pinch of home somewhere within the recipe.

The title is a play on our home's name while also acknowledging the people that these ideas and recipes came from. Without those people, we wouldn't be here, nurtured by their love and living our lives to the best of our abilities.

While there are only a handful of vegetarian options within this book, many of the recipes can be easily reproduced either without meat or by adding one of many meat substitutes. Where possible, we have made suggestions in order to make these meals meat-free.

We hope that you enjoy this book and all of the recipes that have been collected. Eat, drink, and be merry!

Oven Temperature Conversion Table

Gas	°F	°C	Fan
1	275	140	120
2	300	150	130
3	325	170	150
4	350	180	160
5	375	190	170
6	400	200	180
7	425	220	200
8	450	230	210
9	475	240	220

Shelley's Sweet n' Sour Pork

Serves 4

Ingredients
500g pork fillet, cut into small cubes
2 tbsp rice wine or sherry
1 tbsp light soy sauce
2 tsp cornflour
425g pineapple
1 tbsp sunflower oil
1 red pepper, deseeded and cut into cubes
1 carrot, cut into thin strips
1 bunch spring onions, sliced
For the sauce
1 tbsp tomato ketchup
1 tbsp soft brown sugar
1 tbsp light soy sauce
2 tbsp white wine vinegar
2 tsp cornflour blended with 1 tbsp cold water

Method
1. Place the pork in a bowl and add the sherry or rice wine and soy sauce.

2. Stir well and leave to marinate for 20 mins. Stir in the cornflour. Drain the pineapple from the can and reserve the juice, cut into chunks. Heat the oil in a wok or large frying pan and stir-fry the pork for 3-4 mins until browned and cooked through with no pink showing. Remove from the pan.

3. Add the pepper, carrot, spring onion and pineapple chunks to the pan and cook for a further 2-3 mins. Mix the reserved pineapple juice with the sauce ingredients and add to the pan with the pork. Simmer for 3-4 mins. Serve immediately with egg fried rice or noodles.

Janet's Veggie Stew

Serves 4

Ingredients
1 tbsp olive oil
1 onion, peeled and sliced
2 carrots, peeled and diced
2 parsnips, peeled and diced
2 celery stalks, chopped
250g (8oz) swede, peeled and diced
600ml (1 pint) hot vegetable stock
400g can tomatoes
420g can butter beans, drained
A handful of chopped parsley

Method
1. Heat the oil in a large pan, add the onion and fry slowly for 5 minutes. Add the other vegetables, cover and fry over a medium heat for 5 minutes, so they start to soften.

2. Pour in the stock and canned tomatoes, bring to the boil, cover and simmer for 10 minutes. Stir in the beans and cook for another 5 minutes, until the vegetables are tender.

3. Sprinkle the vegetable stew with chopped parsley to serve.

Betty C's Fish Pie

Serves 6

Ingredients

750g (1½lb) floury potatoes, peeled and cut into large chunks
Pinch of salt
2 egg yolks
60g (2½oz) butter
200ml (7fl oz) milk
1tbsp plain flour
175ml (6fl oz) fish stock
200ml (7fl oz) crème fraîche
1tbsp chopped fresh tarragon
Zest of ½ a lemon
750g (1½lb) fish pie mix

Method

1. Place the potatoes in a saucepan and cover with water. Add a large pinch of salt and bring to the boil. Gently simmer, partially covered with a lid, for about 20 minutes, or until the potatoes are completely tender. Drain thoroughly and return the potatoes to the pan over a low heat for a couple of minutes to steam off any remaining water. Use a potato ricer or masher to mash the potatoes. Beat in the egg yolks, 25g (1oz) butter and 50ml (2fl oz) milk and season to taste with freshly ground black pepper and salt.

2. Preheat oven to Gas Mark 4, 180°C, fan 160°C. Place the remaining butter in a small saucepan along with the milk, the flour and fish stock and gently bring to the boil, whisking constantly. Keep whisking as the mixture boils and thickens to form a smooth sauce. Simmer for 3 minutes. Remove from the

heat and stir in the crème fraîche, tarragon and lemon zest and season with plenty of pepper and just a little salt.

3. Have a quick check for bones and then distribute the fish mix over the base of a medium, ovenproof dish. Pour the sauce evenly over the fish and spread the mash over the top, working from the outside in. Use a fork to rake over the top, creating a rough surface. Bake for 35 minutes, or until golden on top and bubbling beneath.

Freezing and defrosting guidelines
Once the dish has cooled completely, transfer it to an airtight, freezer-safe container, seal and freeze for up to 1-3 months. To serve, defrost thoroughly in the fridge overnight before reheating. Loosely cover with foil and bake until dish is thoroughly heated through. Reheat until piping hot.

David's Shepherd's Pie

Serves 4

Ingredients

1 tbsp olive oil
1 onion, finely chopped
1 carrot, finely chopped
1 celery stick, finely chopped
1 garlic clove, finely chopped
500g lamb mince
1 tbsp plain flour
1 tbsp tomato purée
275ml lamb or vegetable stock
1 bay leaf
1 tsp Worcestershire sauce
450g potatoes, chopped into 2cm chunks
200ml milk
50g unsalted butter
pinch of white pepper
green salad or steamed broccoli, to serve (optional)

Method

1. Heat the oil in a large pan over a medium heat. Add the onion, carrot, celery and garlic, and sauté for 5 mins over a medium heat.

2. Add the lamb mince to the pan and use a wooden spoon or spatula to break it up. Cook until well browned, stirring regularly, then sprinkle in the flour and mix well. Add the tomato purée, stock, bay leaf, Worcestershire sauce and seasoning to taste. Mix everything together well, cover with a lid and simmer for 30 mins, stirring from time to time.

3. Meanwhile, put the potatoes in a separate pan and cover with

hot water. Place over a medium heat and simmer for 20 mins or until tender and cooked through. Drain, then return to the pan and shake over a low heat to steam off excess moisture.

4. Put the milk in a small pan and heat gently over a low heat. Remove the potatoes from the heat and crush with a potato masher until smooth. Add the hot milk, butter and white pepper, and beat until fluffy and well blended.

5. Preheat the oven to gas 5, 190°C, fan 170°C. Remove the bay leaf from the lamb mixture and transfer to a large ovenproof dish. Spoon the mashed potato on top and use a fork to spread it around, sealing in the meat and making a stripy pattern.

6. Bake in the oven for 30 mins until the potato is crisp and golden on top. Serve with a green salad or steamed broccoli, if you like.

Tip: Try sprinkling some grated cheese evenly over the mashed potato before baking, or chop some parsley and sprinkle over the shepherd's pie before serving.

Vegetarian option: Substitute the lamb for plant based mince and use vegetable stock for the gravy.

"First, we eat. Then, we do everything else."
Ernestine Ulmer

John's Chicken Curry

Serves 8

Ingredients

3 tbsp vegetable oil
900g boneless chicken thigh fillets
1 onion, sliced
2 red peppers, deseeded and chopped
2½ piece root ginger, peeled and chopped
2 cloves garlic
6 tbsp Tikka Masala or medium curry paste
For the prawns
1 tbsp tamarind paste
2 x 400g can chopped tomatoes
300ml chicken stock
225g tinned chickpeas
1 tsp caster sugar
3 tbsp chopped fresh coriander
Rice, to serve

Method

1. Cut each chicken thigh fillet into four. Heat 2 tbsp of the oil in a large frying pan or wok, add the chicken and sauté over a high heat for 10 mins or until golden. Transfer to a plate.

2. Add the remaining oil, onions and peppers to the pan and sauté for 3 mins or until soft.

3. Stir in the ginger, garlic, Tikka Masala and tamarind pastes and cook for 1 min.

4. Add the chicken, tomatoes, chicken stock and chickpeas, then bring to the boil. Cover and simmer for 20 mins or until the chicken is tender but cooked through with no pink showing.

5. Remove the lid and simmer uncovered for a further 10 mins or until the sauce has thickened slightly.

6. Stir in the sugar and season to taste. Stir in the coriander and serve with rice.

Elaine's Cod Loins in Tomato Sauce

Serves 2

Ingredients

2 cod loins
4 leeks
1 red pepper
3 spring onions
1 vegetable golden rice
1 tin of sweet corn

Method

1. Parcel the cod loins with the spring onions in tin foil and put into the oven on 200 degrees celsius for 45 minutes. Check back after 45 minutes and, if needs be, put the cod back in for 15 minutes or until the fish falls apart.

2. Chop up the leeks, pepper, and onions and steam. Add to rice when cooked and add in the tinned sweetcorn.

3. Serve the rice with the peppers, sweet corn, and spring onions round the plate.

4. Put steamed leeks in the middle of the plate and place cod loins on top.

5. Heat up tomato sauce (either homemade or shop bought) and pour over the top.

6. Add a little pepper on top and enjoy!

Mary's Steak and Ale Pie

Serves 6

Ingredients

375g sheet puff pastry
1 medium egg, beaten
For the beef casserole
900g pack lean diced beef
3 tbsp plain flour
1 large onion, finely sliced
3 celery sticks, finely chopped
5 thyme sprigs
1½ tbsp tomato purée
2 tsp caster sugar
750ml pale ale
1 beef stock cube, crumbled
500g chestnut mushrooms, thickly sliced
1½ tbsp grainy mustard

Method

1. Preheat the oven to gas 2, 150°C, fan 130°C. Put the beef in a mixing bowl with the flour and some salt and toss to coat. Transfer to a lidded, flameproof casserole dish and add the onion, celery, thyme, tomato purée, sugar, ale and the stock. Season, bring to a simmer on the hob, then put the lid on, transfer to the oven and cook for 3 hrs, adding the mushrooms for the final hour, or until the beef is completely tender.

2. Once the meat is properly cooked, remove the casserole from the oven, and put back on the hob. Add the mustard and bring to a simmer and cook, lid off, for 10-15 mins until the sauce is reduced to your preferred consistency (if you're serving with mash, we recommend keeping it quite saucy). Transfer to a rectangular pie dish, roughly 30cm x 20cm, and leave to cool to

room temperature.

3. Once cool, preheat the oven to gas 6, 200°C, fan 180°C. Unroll the pastry and cut out a rectangle slightly larger than the pie dish. Wet the edges of the pie dish with water, then drape the pastry over the top and press down to secure them. Brush the pastry on the pie all over with beaten egg.

4. Place on a baking tray and bake in the oven for 30-40 mins, covering the pastry loosely with kitchen foil if it's getting too dark, until the filling is bubbling up over the sides. Remove from the oven, leave to stand for 5 mins, then serve.

Tip: To make this alcohol free, just replace the ale with a further beef stock cube made up to 500ml.

Louise's Lasagna

Serves 4-6

Ingredients

1 tbsp olive oil
1 onion, diced
1 carrot, diced
1 celery stalk, diced
2 garlic cloves, finely sliced
250g beef mince
250g pork mince
1 tbsp tomato purée
400g tin chopped tomatoes
200ml beef stock
200ml red wine
1 tsp Worcestershire sauce
9-12 lasagne sheets (depending on the size of your baking dish)
50g Parmesan, grated
150g pack mozzarella, shredded
For the white sauce
50g butter
50g plain flour
550ml semi-skimmed milk

Method

1. In a large pan, heat the olive oil over a low heat. Fry the onion, carrot, celery and garlic for 5 mins, or until softened. Add the mince and fry on a medium heat until golden. Turn up the heat, pour in the wine and bubble until reduced. Stir in the tomato purée, chopped tomatoes and stock. Add in the Worcestershire sauce and simmer for 15 mins, or until the liquid has reduced. Season.

2. Meanwhile, make the white sauce. Melt the butter in a small

saucepan over a low heat and add the flour. Whisk until combined and cook on low for 1-2 mins. Remove from the heat and gradually whisk in the milk until you have a loose sauce. Season. Return to a gentle heat and whisk constantly until the sauce thickens.

3. Preheat the oven to gas 6, 200°C, fan 180°C. Layer up the lasagne in a baking dish, starting with a third each of the ragu, then the pasta, then the white sauce. Repeat twice. Top with the Parmesan and mozzarella then bake in the oven for 40-45 mins, until piping hot and crisp and bubbling on top. Serve immediately.

Vegetarian option: Substitute the mince for a meat free mince and use vegetable stock instead of beef.

Tony's Mushroom Soup

Serves 4

Ingredients

1 tbsp olive oil
1 onion, finely chopped
750g chestnut mushrooms, sliced
2 garlic cloves, crushed
500ml vegetable stock
100ml milk
2 tbsp chopped fresh parsley
Drizzle of extra virgin olive oil

Method

1. Heat the oil in a large saucepan over a medium-high heat. Add the onion and cook for 5 mins until starting to soften. Add the mushrooms, increase the heat to high and cook for 10 mins until tender and golden, stirring frequently. Add the garlic and cook for 1 min. Remove a large spoonful of the mushrooms and set aside on a plate as garnish.

2. Pour the stock into the pan and bring to the boil. Remove from the heat and blend until smooth using a stick blender.

3. Return the soup to the saucepan, add the milk and heat through. Add more water or stock if your soup is very thick. Season to taste and serve in bowls garnished with the reserved mushrooms, a sprinkling of parsley and a drizzle of olive oil.

"Good food is the foundation of genuine happiness."
Auguste Escoffier

Becca's Pesto Pasta

Serves 2

Ingredients

125g wholemeal fusilli
100g green beans, trimmed and cut in half
4-5 tbsp green pesto, to taste
100g cherry tomatoes, halved
1 tbsp olive oil
Handful fresh basil, shredded

Method

1. Bring a large pan of salted water to the boil and cook the pasta for 10 mins for al dente. Add the green beans to the pan for the last 4 mins of cooking.

2. Drain the pasta and veg and tip back into the saucepan. Add the pesto, cherry tomatoes and olive oil. Mix well to coat the pasta. Sprinkle with basil leaves to serve.

Mel's BBQ Pork Nachos

Serves 6

Ingredients

250-300g leftover roast pork, torn or chopped up
200g bag Tesco cool tortilla chips
185g smoked Cheddar, grated
1 fresh chilli, finely sliced (optional)
Lime wedges, to serve (optional)
For the homemade BBQ sauce
200ml tomato ketchup
60ml cider vinegar
2 tbsp dark brown sugar
1 tsp Worcestershire sauce
For the slaw
½ large pointed cabbage, or ½ red cabbage, very finely shredded
2 carrots, grated
3 tbsp sour cream and chive dip
3 tbsp half-fat crème fraîche
30g fresh coriander, chopped
4 spring onions, sliced, plus 2 extra to serve on top of nachos

Method

1. Preheat the oven to gas 7, 220°C, fan 200°C Fan. To make the sauce, mix the ketchup, vinegar, sugar, Worcestershire sauce and maple syrup in a large bowl. Add the pork and toss through to coat.

2. Scatter half the tortilla chips over the base of a large ovenproof dish or roasting tin. Top with half of the grated cheese, then repeat the layers and top with the pork and BBQ sauce, leaving a few tbsp sauce to drizzle over at the end.

3. Bake in the oven for 12-15 mins until the cheese has just

melted and pork is hot through.

4. While the nachos are baking, make the slaw: mix all the ingredients (except the extra spring onions) well, then add a few tbsp water to loosen the dressing if needed.

5. Remove the nachos from the oven and top with chilli, if using, and the extra sliced spring onions.

6. Serve the nachos warm with the fresh slaw on the side and lime wedges to squeeze over, if you like.

Clive's Roast Beef with Horseradish Mash

Serves 2 with leftovers

Ingredients

500g roasting beef joint
2 tsp Dijon mustard
1 tsp horseradish sauce
1 tbsp vegetable oil
400g Maris Piper potatoes, peeled and diced
30ml semi-skimmed milk
25g butter
1 tbsp creamed horseradish
2 frozen Yorkshire puddings
150g asparagus
150g Tenderstem broccoli
For the gravy
1 tbsp plain flour
1 tbsp redcurrant jelly
100ml red wine
½ beef stock cube, made up to 200ml

Method

1. Preheat the oven to gas 6, 200°C, fan 180°C. Rub the beef with the mustard and horseradish; season generously. Heat the oil in a large frying pan until nearly smoking, then add the beef joint and sear for 1 min each side. Transfer the joint to a roasting tin and roast for 25-45 mins, depending how well done you prefer it cooked. Cover loosely with foil.

2. Meanwhile, put the potatoes in a large saucepan, cover with water, bring to the boil, then simmer for 20 mins until tender. Season and add the milk, butter and horseradish, then mash until very smooth.

3. For the gravy, pour any beef juices into a saucepan and stir in the flour and redcurrant jelly. Cook over a medium heat for 1 min, then add the wine. Turn up the heat, whisking all the time. After 2 mins, stir in the stock. Simmer for 5-10 mins, stirring regularly; season to taste.

4. Meanwhile, put the Yorkshire puddings on a tray and cook to pack instructions. Bring a pan of water to the boil and cook the vegetables for 3-4 mins until al dente.

5. Carve the beef into slices and serve with the mash, Yorkshires, vegetables and gravy for a simple and delicious roast for two.

Linda's Best Burger Ever!

Ingredients

1 small onion, finely chopped
1 garlic clove, finely chopped
6 x thyme sprigs, leaves picked and chopped
600g beef mince (minimum 15% fat)
1 egg yolk
1½ tsp English mustard, plus extra for spreading
50g Parmesan, finely grated
4 rashers smoked streaky bacon
4 thin slices mature Cheddar
4 brioche burger buns, cut in half
6 iceberg lettuce leaves, chopped
1 beef tomato, sliced into 8
4 tsp tomato ketchup

For the pickled cucumber
½ cucumber, thinly sliced
50ml white wine vinegar
2 tsp caster sugar
½ tsp mustard seeds

For the coleslaw
¼ white cabbage, sliced
½ carrot, grated
¼ onion, finely chopped
½ tbsp mayonnaise
1 tbsp crème fraîche
Few chives, chopped

Method

1. To make the pickled cucumber, put the sliced cucumber in a bowl. Sprinkle with ¼ tsp salt, toss to combine and leave for 15 mins. Rinse and squeeze out any excess water. Meanwhile, heat

the vinegar, sugar and mustard seeds in a small pan for 2-3 mins, until the sugar has dissolved. Remove from the heat and pour over the cucumber. Leave for at least 15 mins, or overnight, if possible. Store the pickle in a lidded container in the fridge until ready to use (it will keep for up to 1 week).

2. To make the coleslaw, mix the cabbage, carrot and onion in a bowl. Stir through the mayonnaise, crème fraîche and chopped chives. Season to taste, then cover and set aside in the fridge while you make the burger.

3. In a bowl, combine the onion, garlic, thyme and beef mince with the egg yolk, mustard, Parmesan and a little seasoning. Mix thoroughly, then form into 4 thick patties (just smaller than the diameter of the bun).

4. Preheat the barbecue to medium-high and cook the bacon for 2 mins on each side, or until crisp and golden. Remove and set aside.

5. Cook the burgers for 5 mins on one side, until golden. Turn them over, put the cheese on top and close the barbecue lid (or cover with a metal container if your barbecue doesn't have a lid) to help the cheese melt. Cook for 5 mins, or until the burgers are cooked through.

6. Meanwhile, toast the cut sides of the brioche bun halves on the barbecue bars. Put the bottom bun halves on a board, top each with lettuce, tomato, a beef patty, a slice of bacon and a portion each of pickled cucumber and coleslaw. Spread the ketchup and mustard onto the top bun halves, then add to the top of the burger stack. Put a skewer through the top of the burger to hold it all together when serving.

Vegetarian option: Use plant based burgers. Remove the bacon or use a vegetarian alternative.

Rach's Chicken and Leeks in White Wine Sauce

Serves 4

Ingredients

1 tablespoon olive oil
500 grams boneless skinless chicken breasts
¼ teaspoon salt
¼ teaspoon pepper
4 slices bacon, chopped
1 large leek, sliced into thin half moons (white and light green parts) and washed thoroughly
225 grams white mushrooms, sliced
60ml dry white wine (such as chardonnay, pinot grigio)
230ml heavy cream
100 grams parmesan cheese

Method

1. In a large, deep skillet, heat olive oil over medium heat. Add chicken and cook for 8 minutes on one side before flipping and cooking for an additional 8 minutes or until cooked through (internal temperature of 165°F). Remove to a plate.

2. To the pan, add bacon and cook until crispy. Remove bacon to a paper towel lined plate, keeping grease in pan.

3. Add leeks to bacon grease and cook until starting to soften. Add mushrooms and continue to stir and cook until mushrooms are browned and cooked. Add white wine and increase heat to medium-high. Cook until liquid is reduced by about half.

4. Reduce heat to medium and add cream and parmesan cheese. Simmer until thickened, then add chicken and bacon back to the pan. Serve immediately.

"The only thing I like better than talking about food is eating."
John Walters

Kim's Pork Roast

Serves 8

Ingredients

2kg large pork leg joint with rind
3 garlic cloves, sliced
15g fresh sage, leaves finely sliced
3 large onions, thickly sliced
2 tbsp vegetable oil
1 tbsp sea salt flakes

Method

1. Remove the pork from its packaging 2 hrs before cooking and dry really well with kitchen paper. Keeping the string on, use a very sharp knife to score the skin 10-12 times, going through to the fat but not the meat. Leave to dry, uncovered, on a plate in the fridge for 1½ hrs, then allow to come to room temperature for 30 mins.

2. Preheat the oven to gas 8, 230°C, fan 210°C. Put the pork, skin-side down, on a board and use a small knife to make deep holes in the meat all over. Push a few slices of garlic and some sage into each hole, then season lightly.

3. Put the onions in the base of a shallow roasting tin and put the pork on top, skin-side up (the meat should rise above the sides). Rub the oil all over the meat and skin; evenly sprinkle the sea salt over the skin. Add enough water (400- 500ml) to cover the base of the tin, taking care not to wet the pork skin.

4. Roast for 25 mins. Reduce the heat to gas 4, 180°C, fan 160°C; roast for a further 2 hrs. Top up with water if necessary so the onions don't catch.

5. If the crackling isn't crisp and golden after 2 hrs, increase the heat to gas 8, 230°C, fan 210°C, and cook for another 10 mins or so. Once crisp, cover loosely with foil and set aside to rest for 20 mins.

Tip: Drying is important because you need the skin to be completely dry for the oil to stick to it. Any moisture will stop the crackling developing.

Anne's Chicken Salad

Serves 6

Ingredients

1½ tsp smoked paprika
1 vegetable stock cube, crumbled
2 thyme sprigs, leaves picked
3 chicken breasts
1 large echalion shallot, thinly sliced into rounds
4 tbsp sherry vinegar or red wine vinegar
80g sun-dried tomatoes, roughly chopped, plus 5 tbsp oil from the jar
1 tbsp Dijon mustard
1 avocado, diced
½ cucumber, cut into half-moons
200g cherry tomatoes, halved
170g pack classic crispy salad leaves
20g fresh basil, leaves picked
20g Parmesan, shaved

Method

1. Mix the paprika, crumbled stock and thyme in a small bowl. Sprinkle over the chicken, then cover and set aside for at least 10 mins, or overnight in the fridge.

2. Put the shallots in a bowl with the vinegar, season with salt and scrunch well with your hands to mix. Set aside to lightly pickle.

3. Heat 1 tbsp sun-dried tomato oil in a large frying pan over a medium heat. Cook the chicken breasts for 3-4 mins until golden, then fl ip and cook for a further 3-4 mins until cooked through. Set aside to rest. Splash 2 tbsp water into the pan, scraping up all the bits; reserve the liquid. Thinly slice the

chicken.

4. Pour the vinegar and pickled shallots into a large bowl (or a container if making for a picnic). Add 4 tbsp sun-dried tomato oil with the mustard and reserved chicken pan juices; stir well to combine and season with pepper.

5. Layer up the salad starting with the avocado, sun-dried tomatoes, cucumber and cherry tomatoes, followed by the chicken, lettuce, basil leaves and Parmesan on top. Toss everything together when ready to serve.

Vegetarian option: Use plant based chicken breasts to create this wonderful salad!

Tree's Crispy Beef Stir Fry

Serves 4

Ingredients

240g long grain rice
100ml vegetable oil
2 tbsp cornflour
1½ tsp Chinese five spice
340g pack beef medallion steaks, cut into ¼cm thick strips
1½ tbsp soy sauce
2 limes, juiced
1 tbsp sweet chilli sauce
2 tsp sesame oil
1 red chilli, halved, seeded and sliced
20g ginger, peeled and finely sliced
2 garlic cloves, peeled and finely sliced
1 yellow pepper, finely sliced
206g pack curly kale

Method

1. Cook the rice following the pack instructions, then set aside.

2. Heat the vegetable oil in a wok until almost smoking. Meanwhile, combine the cornflour, Chinese five spice and a pinch of salt in a bowl. Toss the strips of beef in the cornflour mixture to coat.

3. In a bowl, mix the soy, lime juice and chilli sauce, then set aside.

4. Cook the beef in the wok in two batches, each for 2-3 mins, until golden and crispy. Transfer to kitchen paper to drain and discard the oil. Once finished, discard any vegetable oil left in the wok.

5. Heat the sesame oil in the wok over a medium-high heat, then add the chilli, ginger and garlic. Cook for 30 secs, then add the pepper and cook for 2 mins, stirring often. Add the kale and cook for a further 2-3 mins, stirring often, until it has wilted.

6. Return the beef and the soy mixture to the wok. Cook for 2-3 mins, then serve with the rice.

Christine's Toad in the Hole

Serves 4

Ingredients

75g plain flour
2 eggs
100ml milk
3tbsp vegetable oil
8 chipolatas
4 sage leaves
For the gravy
1 large onion, thinly sliced
1 heaped tbsp plain flour
500ml (17fl oz) dry cider
1 tsp mustard
Peas, to serve (optional)

Method

1. Preheat the oven to gas 8, 230°C, fan 210°C. To make the batter, put the flour, eggs and milk in a small blender with a pinch of salt and pepper and whizz until smooth.

2. Heat 2 tablespoons of the oil in a 4-hole Yorkshire pudding tin on the hob and briefly brown the chipolatas, two in each hole. Pour the batter into the hot tin, around the chipolatas, and top each hole with a sage leaf. Cook in the oven for 15-20 minutes.

3. Meanwhile, make the gravy. Heat the remaining 1 tablespoon of oil in a large frying pan and cook the onion for about 5 minutes until softened and golden brown. Stir in the flour, cook for 1 minute, then add the cider. Stir well, scraping up all the flour. Add both mustards and bring to the boil, and cook for a further 5 minutes until thickened. Season. Serve with the toad in the

holes and some peas, if you like.

Vegetarian option: Meat-free sausages are a great alternative for this heartwarming recipe!

"I cook with wine. Sometimes I even add it to the food."
W.C. Fields

Betty T's Spanish Chicken

Serves 4

Ingredients

1 tbsp olive oil
8 chicken thighs
125g chorizo
1 onion, sliced
2 garlic cloves, sliced
100ml dry white wine (optional)
400g tin chopped tomatoes
400g tin cannellini beans, washed and drained
1 sprig thyme

Method

1. Heat the oil in a large pot with lid. Cook the chicken thighs for 5 mins on each side. Remove from the pot. Thickly slice the chorizo, then cook it for a couple of minutes until starting to brown, then tip in the onion and garlic, and cook for 5 mins.

2. Add the wine (if using) and simmer until nearly boiled away. Tip in the tomatoes and beans, 200ml water and season. Return the meat to the pot and add the thyme.

3. Simmer for 30-35 mins with lid on (top the stew up with water if it looks like it's becoming dry) until cooked. Cut into a thick chunk of chicken to check that it is cooked through.

Brian's Roast Chicken

Serves 4-5

Ingredients

1 whole chicken, about 1.7kg
1 garlic bulb, unpeeled, halved horizontally
1 lemon, halved, plus a squeeze for the gravy
A handful of thyme sprigs
5 fresh bay leaves
125g soft unsalted butter
About 2 tbsp extra-virgin olive oil
100ml white wine
3 tbsp plain flour
About 400ml fresh chicken stock

Method

1. Preheat the oven to 200°C, fan 180°C, gas 6. Fill the chicken cavity with half a bulb of garlic, half a lemon and the herbs. Season all over with flaky salt and black pepper.

2. Pack the butter under the skin on the breast and legs. Place the chicken in a roasting tin, drizzle the oil over the skin, squeeze over the other lemon half and maybe season a bit more. Tuck the other half of the garlic bulb in, too.

3. Roast for 15 minutes, then turn the oven down to 180°C, fan 160°C, gas 4 and roast for a further 45 minutes. Check the bird is cooked by spearing between the leg and the breast with a skewer and if any pinkness appears, carry on cooking. Once cooked, leave to rest for 15 minutes; prop the bird up to let the juices run out.

4. Pour the juices from the roasting tin into a jug and skim off as much of the fat as is practical. Pour the white wine into the

roasting tin and stir to release all the lovely sticky bits from the bottom. Scrape into a saucepan and add the roasting juices. Whisk in the plain flour and cook for a minute, then gradually whisk in the chicken stock to your preferred thickness. Simmer for 5-10 minutes. Add a squeeze of lemon juice and season to taste.

5. To serve, joint the bird into about 10 pieces and place on a platter, then pour the gravy over the meat.

Asfati's Brinjal Bhaji

Serves 4

Ingredients

500g of aubergine, whole
2 tbsp of vegetable oil
1 tbsp of onion seeds
1 tbsp of ginger, finely chopped
2 green chillies, chopped
100g of onion, sliced
100g of tomatoes, chopped
1 tsp turmeric powder
1 tsp garam masala
1 tsp red chilli powder
100g of peas, blanched
coriander cress, optional

Method

1. Preheat the oven to 180°C/gas mark 4.

2. Roast the aubergine in the oven or in a tandoor until completely soft. Peel away the skin and roughly chop the aubergine.

3. Heat the oil in a saucepan, add the onion seeds and sauté until they crackle. Add the ginger and green chilli and sauté over a medium heat until the ginger is golden.

4. Add the onions and cook for 3–5 minutes, or until soft. Add the chopped tomatoes and stir in the powdered spices.

5. Mix through the aubergine flesh and peas and heat through. Taste, adjust the seasoning as needed and serve with a garnish of coriander cress.

Betty C's Slow Cooked Liver and Onions

Serves 4

Ingredients

2 tbsp unsalted butter
4 rashers smoked back bacon, cut into strips
450g pack sliced lamb's liver
3 tbsp plain flour
1 onion, thinly sliced
1 beef stock cube, made up to 500ml
1 tsp Worcestershire sauce
1 bay leaf
Mashed potato and peas, to serve (optional)

Method

1. Heat a nonstick frying pan with half the butter over a medium heat and fry the bacon for 3-4 mins until crispy. Remove with a slotted spoon and set aside on kitchen paper.

2. Pat dry the livers, then toss with 2 tbsp flour and plenty of seasoning. Shake of any excess, then cook in the bacon fat over a medium heat for 1-2 mins each side until browned. Set aside.

3. Add the remaining butter to the pan with the onion and cook for 8-10 mins over a medium-low heat until lightly golden. Stir in the bacon and liver.

4. Mix the remaining flour with 2 tbsp stock. Transfer the liver mix to a slow-cooker. Set to low, then pour in the remaining stock, the Worcestershire sauce, bay leaf and the flour paste. Stir well, then cook for 6-8 hrs until the liver is tender and the sauce silky. Serve with mash and peas, if you like.
*Liver is high in vitamin A and should not be consumed by women planning pregnancy or during pregnancy.

Asfati's Lamb Shish Kebabs

Serves 4

Ingredients

1 x 500g lamb neck fillet, cut lengthways into 3 x 10cm (4in) pieces
4 large white pittas
1 tbsp olive oil
1 x 200g tub houmous
2 tbsp Greek style yogurt (optional)
1 tbsp chilli sauce, to serve (optional)
Pickled chilli peppers, to serve (optional)

For the salad
1 x 220g pack cherry tomatoes, halved
1 red onion, thinly sliced
1 cucumber, roughly chopped
Bunch flat-leaf parsley, chopped
2 tsp sumac
1 lemon, juiced

For the pepper paste
1 red pepper, roughly chopped
1 red onion
2 garlic cloves
4 tsp butter
2 tsp chilli flakes
2 tsp ground coriander
2 tsp ground cumin
2 tsp sumac

Method
1. To make the pepper paste, combine the pepper, onion, garlic, butter and the spices and whizz for 2 minutes, or until smooth.

2. Put the lamb in a large bowl and add the pepper paste, rubbing it into the meat until well covered. Set aside for 10 minutes to marinate.

3. Meanwhile, make the salad. Combine the tomatoes, red onion, cucumber and parsley in a large bowl. Add the sumac and lemon juice; toss to combine. Set aside until needed.

4. Preheat a griddle pan. Cook the lamb for 4-6 minutes on each side, until cooked through. Remove and leave to rest, covered with kitchen foil.

5. Wipe the griddle clean with kitchen towel. Brush the pitta with the oil and toast on the griddle for 1-2 minutes, until warmed through.

6. To assemble, put a piece of lamb on each pitta and top with the salad, a little houmous, yoghurt and chilli sauce (if using). Serve with a pickled chilli pepper on the side, if you like.

Lesley's Spaghetti Bolognaise

Serves 4

Ingredients

2 tbsp olive oil
1 onion, finely chopped
2 garlic cloves, finely chopped
500g lean beef
400g tin chopped tomatoes
150ml red wine
1 bay leaf
300g spaghetti
50g Parmesan, grated

Method

1. Heat the oil in a large saucepan over a low heat and fry the onion and garlic for 5 mins, stirring occasionally. Add the mince, increase the heat to medium-high. Cook for 5 mins until well browned, stirring to break it up.

2. Stir in the tomatoes, wine and bay leaf. Bring to the boil, then simmer for 15 mins, stirring occasionally. Cover and cook for 5 mins or until thickened. Season.

3. Meanwhile, bring a large pan of salted water to the boil and cook the spaghetti to pack instructions. Drain, then stir into the sauce. Remove the bay leaf, then divide the Bolognese between 4 bowls and top with the Parmesan.

Vegetarian option: Use one of the many plant based minces to make this a great meat-free dish!

"Dessert is not a meal; it's a moment."
Anh Luu

DESSERTS

Barbara's Slow Cooked Rice Pudding

Serves 6

Ingredients

150g pudding rice
400ml coconut milk
500ml semi-skimmed or whole milk
60g caster sugar
6 cardamom pods, seeds removed and crushed (optional)
425g tin mango slices, drained and diced
1 lime, zested and juiced
20g toasted flaked almonds

Method

1. Preheat the oven to gas 1, 140°C, fan 120°C. Put the pudding rice in a pan over low-medium heat with the coconut milk, milk, sugar and cardamom (if using). Simmer gently for 10 mins. Transfer to a 1.3ltr baking dish and bake for 40 mins or until the rice is tender. Set aside for 10 mins to cool slightly. it will look a little loose when you remove it from the oven but will thicken as it cools.

2. Spoon into serving bowls and top with the diced mango and lime zest. Squeeze over a little lime juice and top with the almonds to serve.

Get ahead: The rice pudding can be made up to 1 day ahead and kept in the fridge.

Betty C's Bread and Butter Pudding

Serves 6

Ingredients

60g lightly salted butter, softened
10 slices thinly sliced white bread, preferably a day old (cut the crusts off if you like)
60g (2oz) sultanas
½ lemon, finely grated zest only
350ml whole milk
100ml double cream
3 eggs
60g (2oz) golden caster sugar
1 tsp vanilla extract
Grated fresh nutmeg

Method

1. Preheat the oven to 180°C, fan 160°C gas 4. Lightly butter a medium baking dish (approximately 20cm x 25cm) with 10g of the butter. Spread the remaining butter generously over one side of the bread slices. Cut each slice into quarters.

2. Arrange half the bread quarters, buttered sides up, over the base of the buttered dish and scatter with half the sultanas and lemon zest. Repeat to use up all the buttered bread, sultanas and lemon zest.

3. Heat the milk and cream together in a small saucepan until steaming hot. Meanwhile, whisk the eggs with 50g of the golden caster sugar, until pale and thick. Slowly pour the hot milk mixture onto the eggs, whisking constantly. Strain through a sieve into a jug, then stir in the vanilla extract.

4. Slowly pour the custard over the bread pudding, being

careful to soak all the bread. Scatter the surface with the remaining sugar and grate over a little nutmeg. Bake for 35-40 minutes in the centre of the oven, until golden brown. Let the pudding rest for 5-10 minutes before serving.

Freezing and defrosting guidelines
Suitable for freezing when raw or cooked (wrap the dish containing the uncooked or cooked pudding in clingfilm and freeze for up to 3 months. Defrost in the fridge overnight and either proceed with cooking the pudding (if uncooked) or heat through for 20 minutes at 160°C, 140°C fan, gas 3 if cooked.

Barbara's Creme Caramel

Serves 6

Ingredients

200g caster sugar
3 large eggs, plus 2 yolks
500ml whole milk
1 tsp vanilla bean paste

Method

1. Put 150g sugar in a small pan over a low heat and just cover with water. Let the sugar melt, then increase the heat and bubble until it turns a nutty brown. Divide between 6 x 150ml ramekins. Preheat the oven to gas 3, 170°C, fan 150°C.

2. Meanwhile, whisk the eggs and yolks with 50g sugar. Heat the milk and vanilla in a small pan over a low heat until small bubbles appear. Remove from the heat and gradually pour over the egg mixture, stirring constantly. Set aside for 10–15 mins, then strain through a sieve into a clean jug.

3. Put the caramel-filled ramekins in a roasting tin and divide the strained milk mix between them. Put the roasting tin on the middle shelf of the oven, then fill with enough boiling water to come halfway up the sides of the ramekins. Bake for 15-20 mins or until the tops are set but the custard is still a little wobbly. Carefully remove from the oven and leave to cool in the tin for 20 mins. Chill in the fridge for at least 4 hrs, or overnight, to set.

4. To serve, run a sharp knife around the inside edge of the ramekins, then turn out onto a plate so that the caramel runs out and over the top. They can be made up to 2 days in advance and kept in the fridge until ready to serve.

Betty C's Fruit Pie

Serves 8

Ingredients

1 x 500g frozen shortcrust pastry block, defrosted
1 medium egg, beaten
1 x 500g mixed frozen berries, defrosted
2 tbsp cornflour
1 orange, zested
115g (4oz) golden granulated sugar

Method

1. Preheat the oven to gas 6, 200°C, fan 180°C. On a floured surface, roll out two-thirds of the pastry into a circle to fit a 20cm-wide pie dish. Put into the tin, crimp the edges, then cut off and reserve any excess pastry. Chill for 20 minutes.

2. Roll out the remaining pastry and cut circles with different sized fluted cutters. Place on a floured tray; chill.

3. Remove the pie dish from the fridge. Line with baking paper and baking beans, then bake for 12-15 minutes. Remove the paper and beans, then brush with the beaten egg. Sprinkle over 1/2 tbsp of the sugar and bake for a further 5 minutes.

4. Drain any excess juice from the berries. Put in a bowl, stir in the cornflour, orange zest and 100g (3 1/2oz) of sugar, then pour into the pie dish.

5. Top the pie with the pastry circles, brush with beaten egg and top with the remaining sugar. Bake for 30 minutes, until golden. Leave to cool completely before serving.

Barbara's All Bran Loaf

Ingredients

100g Self Raising Flour
300ml Skimmed Milk
275g Mixed Dried Fruit
100g All Bran Original
Margarine for greasing the tin

Method

1. Preheat the oven to 180°C or gas mark 4.

2. Put Kellogg's All-Bran, sugar and dried fruit into a basin and mix them well together.

3. Stir in milk and leave All-Bran mixture to stand for half an hour.

4. Sieve in the flour, mixing well, and pour mixture into a well greased 2lb (900g) loaf tin.

5. Bake for about 1 hour.

6. Turn out of tin immediately, and allow to cool.

7. Cut into slices and, if liked, spread with butter.

"Food is our common ground; a universal experience."
James Beard

Betty T's Lemon Drizzle Cake

Serves 10

Ingredients

200g unsalted butter, softened
200g caster sugar
4 eggs
1 tsp vanilla extract
2 lemons, zest and juice
200g self-raising flour
50g ground almonds
150g icing sugar
Pinch poppy seeds

Method

1. Preheat the oven to gas 4, 180°C, fan 160°C. Grease and line a 1kg (2lb) loaf tin with nonstick baking paper.

2. In a large bowl, beat together the butter and sugar until light and fluffy. Add the eggs one by one, beating in well. Add the vanilla, and zest and juice of 1 lemon.

3. Fold in the self-raising flour and almonds until well mixed.

4. Pour into the tin and bake for 55-60 mins. Allow to cool in the tin for 15 mins, then remove and let cool completely.

5. Mix the icing sugar with a little lemon juice to make a thick, pourable icing. Spoon over the cake and sprinkle with the poppy seeds.

Clive's Apple Crumble

Serves 4

Ingredients

650g Bramley cooking apples, peeled, cored and diced into small chunks
2 tbsp caster sugar
1 tsp vanilla
110g self-raising flour
40g demerara sugar, plus 1 tbsp for sprinkling
40g cold salted butter, diced
2 tbsp rolled oats
Custard, cream or ice cream to serve

Method

1. Heat oven to gas 6, 200°C, fan 180°C.

2. Place the Bramley apples, caster sugar, vanilla and 1½ tbsp of water in a saucepan and gently cook for a few minutes until the apples have softened. Taste and add a little more sugar if needed, depending on how tart the apples are. Transfer to a greased ovenproof dish.

3. Place the flour, demerara sugar and butter into a mixing bowl and rub with your fingertips until it resembles breadcrumbs. Stir in the oats. Scatter onto the apples and then sprinkle the extra sugar on top. Bake for 40-45 mins until golden and bubbling. Serve with custard, cream or ice cream.

Betty T's Victoria Sponge Cake

Serves 8

Ingredients

160g unsalted butter, softened
160g self-raising flour, sifted
160g caster sugar
3 large eggs, lightly beaten
1 tsp vanilla extract
100ml double cream
125g strawberry jam
1 tbsp icing sugar, for dusting

Method

1. Pre-heat the oven to gas 3, 170°C, fan 150°C. Grease and line 2 x 8 inch (20cm) springform cake tins with nonstick baking paper.

2. In a large mixing bowl, cream together the butter, vanilla extract and sugar using an electric hand held whisk until light and fluffy. Add the lightly beaten egg a tablespoon at a time, beating well between additions, until fully incorporated. Carefully fold the flour in using a large metal spoon and spoon the batter evenly into the two prepared cake tins.

3. Bake for 25-30 minutes until springy to the touch and a cake tester comes out clean when inserted into the centre of the cakes. Remove and allow the tins to cool on a wire rack for 5 minutes before turning out and peeling away the nonstick baking paper.

4. Whip the cream to soft peaks as the cakes cool, then spread the bottom half of the cake with the cream in an even layer.

5. Spread the strawberry jam evenly and carefully on top of the cream. Sandwich the cake with the other half of the cake and transfer it carefully to a serving plate. Dust with the icing sugar and serve.

Richard's Rhubarb Crumble

Serves 6

Ingredients

400g Rhubarb
400g British Strawberries
2 star anise
75g light brown soft sugar
1 large orange, zest and juice
For the topping:
150g porridge oats
100g plain flour
100g chilled butter, diced
2 tbsp clear honey
100g light brown soft sugar
50g Roasted Chopped Hazelnuts

Method

1. Preheat the oven to 180°C, gas mark 4. Place the rhubarb, strawberries, star anise, sugar, orange zest and juice in a large ovenproof dish.

2. Place the oats, flour and butter in a bowl then, using your fingertips, rub in the butter until it resembles breadcrumbs. Add the honey, sugar and hazelnuts then rub together to form small clumps.

3. Scatter the oaty crumble over the fruit. Sit the dish on a baking sheet in the oven and cook for 45 minutes until the fruit is tender, bubbling around the edges and the top is crunchy and golden brown.

Lesley's Eton Mess

Ingredients

Natural Yoghurt
Gooseberries
Blackberries
Blackcurrants
Redcurrants
Redberries
Meringue nests

Method

1. In a bowl combine all of the fruit before mixing in some yoghurt.

2. Crush up the meringue nests

3. Combine the fruit, yoghurt, and meringues and serve.

Betty T's Gooseberry Pie

Serves 6

Ingredients

460g frozen shortcrust pastry sheets, defrosted
800g gooseberries, stemmed
150g caster sugar, plus extra for topping
2 tbsp elderflower cordial
2 tbsp cornflour
1 egg, beaten

Method

1. Use one of the pastry sheets to line the base of an 18cm round pie dish, trimming any excess pastry from the edges; chill for 30 minutes.

2. Meanwhile, heat ½ the gooseberries in a pan with the sugar, cordial and cornflour. Simmer for 8-10 minutes, stirring until thick and most of the berries have broken down. Remove from the heat and stir through the remaining gooseberries. Allow to cool.

3. Preheat the oven to 200°C, gas mark 6. Spoon the gooseberry filling into the lined pie dish. Brush the edges of the pastry with egg, then use the remaining sheet of pastry to top the pie. Trim any excess and crimp the edges of the pastry together with a fork (keep any excess pastry wrapped in the fridge to use in another recipe). Cut a small cross through the centre of the pastry with a knife to allow the steam to escape while cooking. Brush with egg and scatter over 2 tsp sugar.

4. Bake for 30-35 minutes, until the pastry is golden. Cool for 10 minutes before serving.

"Laughter is brightest in the place where the food is."
Irish proverb

Also Available from Roswell Publishing

Non-Fiction

Send in the Congregation – Rachael Gilliver
The Mysterious Wold Newton Triangle – Charles Christian
The Human Element – Rachael Gilliver
You Are Not Broken – Rachael Gilliver

Fiction

Begin the Beguine – Paul Mackintosh
Death of a Doppelganger – Paul Mackintosh
Letters From Montauk – Rachael Gilliver
The High Price of Fame – Rachael Gilliver

Poetry

A Box at the Back of the Junk Shop – Kate Garrett
Deeds – Kate Garrett
Little Gods – Cara L MeKee
Mozinah's Book of Fairy Tales – Mozinah the Seer

Printed in Great Britain
by Amazon